SLOSH

Δ

THINKING

Dr. Michael Vincent Diorio

Contents

Acknowledgements

Ῠ A moment to create time in an endless capsule of appreciation for giving breath to life. A way to intake the air of thought that surrounds the visceral rim of my mind and exhale a way of living that breeds independence. For a perspective that is trapped in a world that has no boundaries and no limits. A sea of chaos comprised of a land of endless branches that peak above the highest mountains. I thank the beauty of life that portends the beauty of the imagination and the concrete and abstract enterprises of a world that surrounds us all. These are the hands of freedom that helped guide me in developing the images for a better way to see nature's infinite creativity and open the trails for a better way to walk about life.

Preface

Look out at your world and see things no person has seen before. Discover and search for the innermost guidance amongst your deepest thoughts. Transgress the given and shuffle through the ideas created inside your imagination to reach new depths of understanding for how you want to live your life. Capture it and own it. This is your view, exclusive and sacred. Many days extending deep into the dark hours of the night have been dedicated to reflecting on the world around me. The views expressed in the pages of this book accommodate anyone who enjoys seeking alternative perspectives for human endeavor. What I lay down in my own thoughts and words is an expression for how I think true happiness can be achieved. SLOSH is not something that can be obtained overnight. It will take many moments of reading and re-reading this book to truly inbreed the ideas of S.L.O.S.H. But, I can assure you that by the end, you will be a different person with a whole new perspective on life. And so, SLOSH is…..

This book is dedicated to my younger sister Lauren, who embodies and demonstrates raw happiness, day in and day out, with only but the purest, most infectious smile and positive attitude towards living a simple life.

"And So It Begins"

The dark skies cast a shadow upon the earth, and the burning moonlight shimmering above the night precipitates a trembling spell on the mind and up your spiral staircase of enlightenment. The end is not near for the sun will rise tomorrow and the limitless end of your query seizes this moment. But within this maze of mental disparity lies the valued secrets of an unknown mystery. This is your sense of smell, potent and dispelling, but rigorously active. Breathe this violent air of understanding and you will uproot a stronger presence. You seek what you enjoy most and pleasure your senses with ambient noise. But the true vision lies just beyond a subtle voice. Divorce yourself from the gripping chains of a world's imagination of who you ought to be and escape into the uncut world of you, untouched and virgin to the eye's beholder. The task at hand is simple but tantalizing—put thought to reflection and break down the mental barriers put in place by the curses of habit and leap out with liberty to explore the deepest holes and the highest peaks. The human thought, and the astonishing rate at which it occurs, may seem transient in time. It comes hard and fast one second and then in the next descends into the dustbin of the past. The meaning behind a thought, however, is sticky for it offers value and sustenance. As time feverishly passes you by, you amalgamate the meaning of one thought with that of another to form chains of thoughtless meaning within yourself. The thought itself then catalyzes a deeper meaning of an idea. But, suddenly, the idea withers away and you're back in the circle of nothingness. Sometimes, we see lots of colors when we look outside, while other times it's just gray. Does color make us see things better, or just disguise what we see from what it really is? Red, green, blue! What if everything is just seen as gray? The lack of Chroma will dispel the natural influence that color has on the mind and for the first time you can connect with just the basics. Then again, wondering is just a thought, transient in time, and since all thoughts become part of the past, you can wake tomorrow with a fresh mind, a fresh thought. "And So It Begins…"

"6 Senses of an Experience"

The next time you look out your window, see with your ears and hear with your nose. It's not often that you have the freedom to just sit back and take the moment. This moment is your moment. No one can take it from you. You're sitting on a sandy beach, the sun is beaming down onto your body like warm hot chocolate on a snowy day and the wind hugs your arms and legs as you drift into a sea of thought and reflection. The sand cleanses your toes like a brisk mist over your face as you lightly twist and turn your feet into the warm and grainy sand particles like they were in a carwash against buffer pads. You are free. This is your moment and no one can take it from you. The sound of the ocean resonates through your ears with fainting presence. You're relaxed, you are free. Not a care in the world. No obligations, no requirements, no financial burdens, just you and this moment. You're lying beneath a tree. It's a warm sunny day with a slight breeze blowing over your cheeks. This tree is your protector, guarding you from all things outside of your thoughts. And you're lying there, beneath this tree, face towards the sky, eyes closed, and this is your moment. You can hear every sound around you. The branches of the tree grazing through the sky, the ants beside you busy at work, and the sound of the rumbling earth below you as it embraces your presence and conforms itself to your body. You are one with nature. Suddenly, a noise to your left grabs your attention. It's the sound of an acorn nut falling from the tree beside you and a squirrel is approaching subtly. This squirrel is not like any ordinary squirrel. It engages your space without any fear or caution, as if you two have been in this position before. You acknowledge the squirrel's presence and he reciprocates graciously. You've never had a relationship with an animal before, but this one seems special because you're at peace and harmony with your thoughts and the world around you. Slowly, you close your eyes and let your mind drift toward the back of your head. You're eyes are reversed, your heart rate is trimming, and you seize the moment with liberty and solitude. This is your moment, and nothing can take it from you. It's moments like these that you must seize and seek out. The stress, the concerns, the mundane routines all become but a distant thought and you can actually sit back and focus on that solitary point in time that is too often put off. Reflection has its advantages and the mind is such a powerful engine that it needs these quintessential moments to reboot and restart. We depend on it, and we all need more of it each day for every single thing that we do in the conscious, timeless world. As long as you are awake, you are experiencing, and every time you flare your senses you can experience something new. Whether you choose to acknowledge it or not, no two days are alike and although each day may seem to be stringed to the quartet of a familiar tune, realize that today is unlike any day before. The challenges that you face are opportunities to be someone different. So make this day different and experience something new. An experience becomes just a part of the distant mind the moment that experience ends and so to try and recall those experiences in the mind is both self-defining and self-limiting. To reflect is to analyze the world for what it is, not to relive the moments that already occurred in our past. Those moments had their chance, and they are gone now. Gone forever! What remains is dust, and so to regain that experience you must wipe away that dust. Beneath, you will find a memory and the mind's poor interpretation of what feeling it had during that past experience. You desperately try, but you always come up short as you attempt to recreate all the details. The problem is that the true emotion and sensation that you are trying to uncover is stuck in the mud where that experience took place. It's embedded within the fossil of that moment. To relive is to recapture. To rehash is to reflect. An experience is temporary and the sensations associated with it are also confined to that moment. Reflection upon an experience is a stubborn mental exercise in trying to dissect the imagination to retrieve those sensations. But focus on the moment of the experience and you can once again become a part of it. There are certain variables of any human experience that exert a more dominant force on the formation of that memory in a way that allows us to recapture that experience better. Is it the smell, the sight, the feel, the hormonal imbalances, or a combination of all of these that makes the experience stick more? It all depends on what you choose to sensitive yourself to the most during the experience. If you're walking through a garden and you're focusing intensely on the magnitude and myriad of aromas filling the air then when you recall that event at a future time you'll recreate what it felt like to smell the roses in that moment. Or perhaps you enjoyed most the anticipation within an anxious flowering bud awaiting its day to sprout. You must utilize each one of your natural senses to gain control over the experience. Each person has a unique approach to how they experience the world, but with more detail and attention to the 6 senses you will be able to experience more in the world around you. What do you focus on in life? What variables of your experiences do you find most memorable. Life is full of patterns, and the human mind tends to adhere to these cyclic patterns of life. We were given 6 human senses to experience the world around us, and if you withhold the use of just one of them, then you are unfortunately denying yourself the opportunity to fully experience that moment. Adhere to these principles granted to you by the natural elements of human physiology and they will guide your mind into the experience of a lifetime. Undress yourself of all the barriers you establish as a society-living member and just be human for once. Smell, Hear, See, Touch, Taste, and Function are the only elements of any human experience you'll ever need to utilize. The mind will use these and more to derive all other meaning.

"Head up, Chin up: New Perspective"

People tend to get so stressed out over the most simplistic of things. We all live by a certain derived routine in life. And it's this constant mundane cycle that keeps you adherent to the merry-go round structure of your life. But what are we all actually doing? Of course, cycles are designed to be continuous, for it's the perpetual element of the cycle that makes it consistent and predictable. Most people find comfort in knowing what comes next, but when it comes to your own behaviors; do you really want to succumb to the confining nature of predictability? The sun rising tomorrow is inevitable, the independently functioning heart contraction is inevitable, but why should we as people be inevitable? Change it up and you shall see how changes around you occur on a second by day basis. Go out into the world today and be a bystander to the morning adventures of others. One person is walking with their head parallel to the street and their entire attention being strictly devoted to a window of experience the size of a hand. Another person is sifting through the pages of a book while simultaneously forfeiting their trust in the hope of an accurate next step. The person doesn't care whether that next step is forward, backward, or into a hole in the ground. And yet others sit and wait at a local bus stop for the world

to come to them. These are the adventures of others.
Adventures, that for better or worse, are not being
experienced at all, but rather just the simple act of
passing time. Is this the predictable behavior we've all
come to expect and accept? This is the cycle of life that
captures us all each day as we head off to school, work,
or fulfill an agenda. It is predictable and you must
change it. If you don't want to conform to the cycle, if
you don't want to be painstakingly predictable, then
you need to wake up and elevate your head to a new
position in life. Put down the book, the cellphone, the
problems, and change your perspective. There are so
many ways in life to do this. Maybe you were going to
were a red shirt today, but instead you decided to put
on a blue one. Maybe you were going to walk east
down the same street you always take to work, but
instead you walked west, even if it added 10 more
minutes to your normal commute. Maybe you listen to
station x on the way to work but today you turned off
the radio and listened to the natural radiofrequency of
thoughts inside of your head. There are so many ways
to change your perspective. We're constantly fighting
this ongoing battle of cycles. Around and around we
all go when it only takes a simple, solitary, self-granted
second to escape it all and just travel in a different
direction in life. Today, don't conform to the normal
natural position your head wants to take in the fully
erected physical self. Instead, tilt your head up so that

your chin becomes your new set of eyes and just look up. Look straight up into the sky and take a deep breath, and for once, in this very moment, absorb every part of life for what it is. You've broken free from the chains of the cycle and escaped the normal dimensions of your box. You've changed your perspective and no one can predict your next move for they can no longer see what you see. There are so many forces controlling what surrounds you that the only thing you can control is your next move. Conscious or not, the next move we all will make is the only thing we can take ownership of. Call it free will, or human liberty, the bottom line is it's yours. Today, during your lunch break, go outside. Look up at the sun. This is your shining armor in the sky and its prescribed energy exhumes every one of your tiny cells. Instead of sitting down at the table where you are forced to maintain an upright position to stay properly seated, lie down on the ground and establish continuity with the laws of gravity. Don't fight with the forces of gravity for it is not a fight you are going to win. For the first time, you can embrace the earth's energy and use it to pull all of your stress into the ground below. Get up, get outside, and spot the largest tree in the horizon. This tree will display the most embracing canopy of branches and leaves, and you should go underneath that tree and lie down on your back. Relinquish your right to resistance for the right to be one with earth. The grounds below will harness all of your bad energy and provide you mental, physical, and emotional support to be stable with yourself. Gravity is such a wonderful force if you utilize it in the right manner. Let the laws of attraction bring you closer to the earth and may the relentless anchorage to hope and relief be infinite.

"Two Innate Qualities of Living"

On average, your heart will beat 40 million times in just a single year. Some days it will race within your chest like a galloping horse while other times it will retire into a platonic state of complacency. Essentially, this remarkable display of a biological phenomenon never stops working for you, and if it did, well, then you probably wouldn't be around much longer to realize it. What this phenomenon demonstrates is just how humanly fragile and mortal we are. It would be nice to think of our life in terms of infiniteness, but the hard reality is someday are biological clocks terminate and the physical body each one of us knows all too well will turn into dark soil compost. We all at one point or another ponder the fate of our afterlife, and the fluttering concepts of life after death, renewable spiritual energy, or transcendence into alternative dimensions serve as the palliative relief to our uncertain fate. But, is an afterlife pacifier necessary to our existence? There will always be a curiosity for humans to know more, to want more, but who says we absolutely need more. Imagine for a second that we could design an experiment to study human behavior relative to complacency with given information. If you take 3 groups of humans and label them red, white, and blue. Group Red is told that there is a supreme being called omniscience and that it controls all humans. Group White is told absolutely nothing. And group Blue is divided into 2 subgroups and half are told that the sun controlled the universe and the other half are told that water controlled the universe. The only other instruction for the experiment was that there were no other instructions. The question is what would each group believe after 10 years' time? The answer is that all groups of the study would have established alternative versions of the original given information. The point being that regardless of how each group started out, they'd all arrive at the same exact endpoint: uncertainty. As humans we all innately have two main instincts that defy consistency within a culture. These are curiosity and defiance. As curious beings we're always going to be challenged by the desire to know more. It's the biggest contributor, and some may argue, the only perpetuator to human innovation and progression. Defiance parallels curiosity because to be curious means to step outside the box, and to step outside the boundaries of your limitations is to directly defy the rules and regulations that may have been instituted upon you by previous influences. You need to be more curious and defiant in life if you want to challenge yourself and reach your absolute full human potential. You must stick your hands outside of your box of comfort and routine and go out into the world and make a new box. This new box must be devoid of 4 corners. No right angles, no 90 degrees, no walls, no barriers. You must establish a life inside of an open box. Challenge yourself each day with the notion that there's more than what is just given to you. If everyone went throughout the world each day accepting what was given to them the previous day then no one would ever think ahead. We'd all be living in the past, in a life that was predetermined and predicated upon a preexistent state of existence. Live for tomorrow, live for the future, whereby uncertainty and unknowingness drives your next couple of steps. Think beyond the world at the top of the mountain and you will find an easy descent throughout your life.

"States of Consciousness"

Look to the sky and you will see a whirlpool of clouds, sucking you in like quicksand. There's no end to the sky that lies above you. It hovers there, watching over you at all times like the mother of all nature that it is. If the sky is the mother of nature then the land is the father. The two combined foster all life forms on earth. With thought and reason you can float into the clouds above. Like a rising balloon with no direction, the sky becomes a safe haven of mental escape. Look deep into the blue horizon and transcend into the mental stratosphere of change. The mind can rise to greater depths of dimensional reality than the physical body can ever attain. Water takes on many forms: liquid, solid, and gas. Amongst these 3 phases of existence, you can see how energy exchanges hands with the environment. The mind, like water, can take on equivalent phases of existence. Liquid, solid, and gaseous states of the mind represent forms of energy changes that you can have as well. Liquid and solid states of the mind can be achieved if you allow decompression of all your thoughts and solidification of others. A vaporized mentality requires perspective. Expressing certain areas of your mind will bring to light the powers of those thoughts and so, if for example you decide to contemplate the action of transcending into the skies above, then the mental consciousness will follow. Your thoughts provide the saddle to carry your consciousness. One does not exist without the other, however, the power and direction of one can pull with it the other. This is the power of our mental capacity to coexist in the partitioned fashion of thoughts and consciousness. But, the two occupy the same mental space in time and so they must be simultaneously coupled to one another. To change from one phase to the next requires complete relaxation of your current state of mind. Drift away into deep reflection and hover above your state of consciousness as you undergo a phase change into another perspective of life. Put mind to thought and fly to the clouds above and your conscious being will assume the feelings of flight. Vaporize your mental thoughts to give breath to imagination and your reality will spread wings of its own.

"Synergy of Mind and Body"

We are not strangers to our confusion. Bewilderment floods all of our minds on a daily basis, and yet most of us carry on, unaltered by this natural internal phenomenon. It's rare to encounter a situation that is just black or white. There's always that gray area of ambiguity. When you look out into the fields of galloping humans spinning around the wheel of life, you will see a plethora of peculiar behavior. Nothing about living in this world is simple or normal. From the moment we wake up to the moment we perish deep into an internal dream state, we are being stimulated. And at the center of it all, is you. The cells that formulate your mind which formulate your thoughts are all that you really have in life. These day to day actions, and the façade of an existence that arrests the standard 9-5 routine that you call life, is just a distorted mirror image reflection of the person you truly are. And what you represent, deep in the internal continuum of a controlled state, actually lies on the opposite side of that mirror. When you wake up today, look into the mirror and ignore the fact that your hair may be disheveled or bedridden, or that your eyes have crusted over due to the prolonged retirement from the previous night's sleep, and just look beyond the physical person that you see in front of you all together. Instead, focus on the one within the reflection you see in the mirror. Look past the light-induced outline of the physical you and harness that moment for just a brief second. This is a moment that you acknowledge what it means to be awake for that split hair of a second's time and connect with your emotional status. Feel your pulsating heart try to explode toward you, and determine if it's operating at a normal, elevated, or depressed state. Perceive your heart's rate as a symbol for the rate at which your mind is working. Feel your stomach pylorus churn to fatigue as it waits in anticipation for the morning meal. Now, take a couple deep, elongated breaths and let the fresh intake of oxygen inflate your lungs and body as you inflate your mind with joy. You are human. These are your functions. Automatic and fluent, and without them you are nothing. Let your mind speak for these actions as you but listen for the energy that pours through your veins. You are operating on this human level on a constant basis and you don't even know it. Imagine if your organs were confused, would your thoughts be automatic. Don't let your thoughts dictate your confusion for it's the actions you acquire in life that make your mind seek clarity. It's a hot day; the sun is hovering over you like a giant laser targeting every inch of your physical surface area. You're perspiring profusely, and slowly using your tongue to tumble the thick desiccated saliva that instigates your mouth. You seek refuge inside your house and look quickly toward the refrigerator to satisfy your desires. Are you confused now? You jump to open the door with liberation and crack open that bottle of water without hesitation. You turn the bottle upside down and dump its enriching, reinvigorating contents down your throat like a rapid, relentless waterfall. You're drinking water. You didn't think about it, you just did. Your mind knew exactly what it wanted and how to achieve it.

You weren't confused at all. So if your mind knows how not to be confused at certain times of life, then why let it be at others. Listen to your body, listen to the signals within and they will dictate the mind's thoughts and likewise the mind's ability to achieve its thoughts in the most resistance-free fashion. Think like you drink water and you will find yourself floating along an endless riverbank.

"Inner Alias"

We all live through the faces of our imagination. Day in and day out we interact with others through an alternative form of our true "self". Each one of us creates many versions of this alternative form of our "self", and we use these alternative forms interchangeably to appease others. The "self" is never truly defined and is constantly changing. The "self" is a dynamic combination of other "selfs" that we have identified in the world around us and electively chosen to mimic. Then, how many different types of qualities and characters can one actually assume in life? Just as there are a finite number of musical combinations that can be generated by any one instrument, or a preset number of 6 character license plate numbers, there too are a limited number of characters that we may acquire to help shape our personalities. Essentially, you take bits and pieces of other "selfs" that you observe in the world and combine them to form your own "self". And so, the "self" that you have created is actually being derived from a pool of very desirable traits and characteristics that appeal to the majority of humans. However, there is an ultimate, universal, "self" character that has evolved over the course of human existence and has become a highlight of attraction. Outgoing, funny, witty, intelligent, friendly, sacrificing, giving, determined, are just a few of the qualities that belong to this universal recipe for the ultimate character. You should take on as many of these universally accepted traits as possible and develop your own hybrid character. You sit on a train on the tour of human perspective and look around at the handful of surrounding people, who sit and occupy a physical body in the form of a human exoskeleton. This handful of 10 people is actually 20-30 people because each person has multiple characters that they assume throughout different parts of their day or even life. It's frightening to think that we can act one way in a certain situation and then completely different in another. What complicates the situation even more is that you can tap into your mind to escape the front barrier that you have established in the "self". You can escape deep into your mind and engage with an inner character that possesses no consequences and has total freedom. This is classified as the "inner alias". It's the version of your "self" that truly defines who you are. It's the version of you that you can truly call your own character because it's not an emulated character reflecting what everyone already desires in the world because it exists inside of your mind. It is the true character of you that bears no rules, no boundaries, and is the animal within you. Animals are unpredictable, and your "inner alias" is private and reserved for you alone. This is your "inner alias" and everything centralized around it is the "inner alibi". Be one with yourself and you will see the world as a reflection of harmony and balance for who you want to be.

"The Decision of a Hope"

The process of decision making in life is not a defined algorithm, for it varies greatly from one person to the next. A decision made in the present is a choice we must live with in the future. The simple fact that we must actively and consciously engage in this process instills a level of frankness within every decision that we then make. Life takes us through a series of split nodes presenting us the option to either go left or go right. Calculated risks' and juggling of the pros and cons, gives us insight into the potential outcomes of our speculation, but until you cross the bridge you will never know what faces you on the other side. We maintain comfort in knowing that life guides us from one step to the next, choosing a path, confiding in our liberties as a free thinking organism. Every solitary decision you make in life impacts you in some way or another and it's the culmination of these decisions over the course of your lifetime that makes your journey unique. If every decision imparts implication onto your life then you must value every decision as an opportunity to impart change on your life. Life is a puzzle and each decision that we make represents just a piece of that puzzle. Some pieces are bigger than other pieces and some pieces are border pieces, but in the end the puzzle depends equally on every single piece. For instance, a border piece type of decision would be to determine what college to attend or what career to pursue. Whereas, a regular piece decision would be whether to walk to class or ride your bike. Sometimes, the pieces of the puzzle are already chosen for you and it is your responsibility to put them together. The challenge is to delineate between different decisions and then to assign a significance factor to that process all along the way. Do I get married now or postpone it until later? Should I buy a house or rent? Being faced with decisions like these seems to be life-changing, but in the linear stream of human existence, this decision is equally important to for instance deciding whether to take one road to work over another. You can never know the true outcome of any decision. However, we must determine whether the simple nature of "choosing" precedes action or causes it. If every choice we had to make stems from a predetermined thought, then that choice becomes a reflection of hope. And therefore, if our decisions are based on hopes, we are no longer making decisions, but rather just pursuing wishful thinking. In other words, our decisions become poor excuses for dreams and thus we start to navigate through life in an image of what we hope will happen. If you choose to drink the cup of dark roasted chocolate coffee sitting on the table next to you right now, are you making the decision to satisfy a desire or are you merely hoping that by pursuing the act of introducing the caffeine chemical into your system you will no longer desire? The choice and the dream are mutually exclusive for that which we think as thoughts of reason are merely thoughts of the creative mind to imagine something it desires. Every decision you make has an introspective origin that is influenced by your perceived notion of that decision's outcome. No two decisions are alike and it is this causative fingerprint that makes each choice significant. We all come from different experiences, shaped by different decision outcomes. But what connects us all, what makes us all fall under the realm of being human is that every time we make a decision, we follow it with reflection. It is only human nature to assign reflection to outcome. With reflection you can acquire insight, and so with time your decision making skills will get stronger. But, why do most of us reflect? Is it because we're unhappy with our choices? Is it because we are constantly comparing our decisions to alternatives? You want to make choices in your life that make reflection fun. You want to make decisions like you tie your shoes. Every day before you put on your shoes you reach over to your dresser and pull out a pair of socks. When was the last time you questioned the reason behind the choice to put on a pair of socks? Probably never, unless of course, it was your first time putting on socks. But today, you accept putting on socks as an automatic gesture of your normal routine. You didn't question the thought, but instead conveniently accepted the decision to put on the socks. The hope or dream associated with the decision to put on those socks was still there but the reflective process was absent. And so, in your life you will come across many opportunities to make decisions, almost on a daily basis, and you want to find a way to make it easier on yourself. Some of those decisions, like putting on your socks, you will not think twice about, whereas other decisions you will follow with intense reflection and scrutiny. The choices you make are infused with allied forces to understand those choices. Nonetheless, the hopes and dreams attached to your decisions remain a constant component of decision making, and so if you can determine your desires and dreams you can most certainly anticipate your behavior and the profound nature behind what you will do next.

"Running From Entropy"

At times, we all just want to take a cold shower. It's a fall Monday morning and the outside air has a brisk chill to it. You step into the bathroom and remove your clothing. You step into the tub and let your feet touch the hard porcelain glazed surface like it was a chilled ice cream slab on a fall day. You support all of your weight on your two feet. Your knees want to buckle for they are weak from a long night's rest but you quickly turn the tub nozzle and look up. You pause, frozen in time, as you await the very first drop of water to fall from above and smack you in the face. You are reborn. At other times, you just want to turn the switch off, and run away. You come home from a routine day. You cannot understand how so many hours have passed and yet you are back right where you started. Back where you belong. You run to the closet and swing open the door with ambitious hope for the unknown. It's dark, it's quiet, and it's just you and the open space beyond the door. You jump in and turn the switch off. You think to yourself in solitude with hope that when you turn on the switch you are in a new room. You open the door and see your new life. What are you hiding from? Where are you running? You become so overwhelmed with the insecurities of life that you find no other solution but to just escape them all. Instead of watching yourself day in and day out drown in your puddle of uncertainty, get up and do something about it. You're running from this life to seek out a previous one, one that you associate with more joyous times. These are the times when you are safe and peaceful because this world is filled with chaos and destruction and you want nothing more than to establish order in your life. Where is this order in a world of disorder? You put on a new pair of shoes and just start running, but what you fail to realize is that the new pair of shoes also has many holes at the bottom of them. You're sinking, falling, with no one to catch or find you. You're kidnapping yourself from yourself in hopes that another form of you will come into your life as a source of retrieval. The shining knight in armor associated with happiness becomes your source of conversion from disorder into order. It provides you peace and breaks the laws of entropy.

"The Art of Abstract Interactions"

What is it about human interaction that excites us? Is it our curious nature to look deep into one's eyes and capture their most cerebral thoughts? Or is human interaction simply a means to pass the time? Each day we succumb to our role as social beings engaging with our surroundings. Most times, those surroundings are other people, while other times it involves inanimate objects like the couch or bed that is probably supporting your body while you currently read this. But what about the other interactions we possess on a daily basis. These "other" interactions are referred to as "abstract interactions" for they do not fall under the normal "noun" category. These types of interactions are not a person, a place, or a thing. Instead they're an inference of something. These "abstract interactions" piggyback off our normal everyday interactions and are, to some degree, hidden or camouflaged within a conversation. Imagine one day you're on your way home from work, and on this particular day you decide to stop off at the bookstore. You walk through the entrance only to be immediately arrested by the new arrivals staring you in the face at the front of the room. You're intrigued, but not to the point of purchase. You subtly continue your way past the best sellers and on to your favorite section: fiction. Your attention peaks towards the eye's delight and you grab a book from one of your favorite authors. You head to the checkout and while standing in line peacefully, the person in front of you turns around and asks "get anything good?". You don't want to be rude so you respectfully respond "just another book to pass the time". You had a social interaction with this person, unwarranted, but still an interaction. It was verbal, it was in the moment, and it was a real human dialogue. But what about the underlying, hidden, "abstract interaction" you didn't even know you had with this person. This involved the thoughts that took place behind the scenes of that awkward ongoing engagement. These thoughts weren't verbalized. The thoughts like "why is he/she asking me this?" or "I really don't like this person's hair!". And yet still, your opponent in the conversation held a completely different set of thoughts that were also not verbally announced. These piggyback thoughts surrounding our interactions with others are the "abstract interactions" and they are a real part of your everyday life whether you acknowledge them or not. The next time you interact with someone, focus on the content of the conversation, but also try to pick up on the "abstract interactions" that are displayed through either your or the other person's nonverbal physical cues. The next time you attempt a conversation with someone; pierce their eyes with yours like an eagles talons around its prey. Most of us overlook this very important tip in successful conversation. A conversation has two main elements to them: one involves enlightenment, and other involves expression of dominance. If we think back to our primitive ancestors and evaluate the importance of communication in their progression as a species, we can illuminate two very important facts: 1. we are social organisms and 2. we can use communication to understand one another's ideas. Now, our ancestors depended on communication to organize affairs and accomplish goals more efficiently. In today's culture, we also use communication to socialize and accomplish goals, but communication takes place at a more frequent rate and on a more diverse spectrum of platforms. With the advent of technology, communication platforms have erupted in many different forms and thus have diminished our need for the one-on-one in person engagement. Go out into the world and look directly into another person's eyes when you speak to them because it will have such a profound impact on the dynamics of your conversations with others. Vision is a two-way street. Our eyes are used to intake visual images of our surroundings so that we can then interact with them. However, when you take part in a one-on-one conversation, you want to limit your acknowledgement of your surroundings as much as possible so as to minimize the depth and quantity of perceived interferences flowing through your retina. Instead, you want to channel your vision directly toward your partner in the conversation, and show that person you're engaged solely and directly into his/her being. By looking directly into one's eyes during the conversation you freeze their mind and make them focus on you as they speak. And when they focus on you, they start focusing on what it is that you could be possibly judging them for. The person will start to question whether you are judging them for things like "is my hair sticking up?" or "do I have food stuck in my teeth?". If that person is so intensely focused on whether or not they are being judged, then they're going to be focused on what they say and how they look saying it and ultimately that will deter them from generating dominance toward you. By locking your eyes against another's you cripple them from being able to talk freely in the conversation because they become so intimidated that they start focusing on what it is that you are judging them for instead of focusing on what it is they are trying to tell you. This is the art of conversing and it begins and ends with the eyes. The unknown and abstract dynamics behind the role-playing act of conversing is what makes it intuitive. You can be anyone and represent anything that you allow your mind to reflect from your body. So let others see you for your internal thoughts and thus allow your conversations with others to be a continuous stream of your personal self-reflection.

"Time and Thought Again"

Time! Stop living by the clock and find your own hands to revolve around. The hours, minutes, and seconds that govern your life are just dead weight holding you back from true peace. Today, you woke up at the same time you wake up every day. You put on your clothes, grabbed something to drink, and off to work you went. You left early to make sure you gave yourself enough time to overcome any delays. You try to reflect on what it is that you value more in life, but you just can't seem to find the time, because you're wrapped up in a tick-tock straight jacket and sinking quick. The rest of your day is already chosen for you as you glance over the schedule and you just can't understand how something as abstract as time could yet be such a large part of your life. Time is what keeps us all adhering to a schedule. But in a universe governed by the principles of entropy how should we be expected to maintain such an orderly structure. Time, after all, is just a projection of some future instance that people accept as guaranteed reality. But our life does not favor the laws of time for time is a funneling motion of progression. Does the universe know time? Sure the planets, the sun, the earth, and the universe all operate within a certain special structure and relationship that we've quantified by the big and little hands of the clock. But if you expurgate the rules of time, and jump into a timeless capsule of your mind, then you start to live for who you are. You don't become associated with a second, a minute, or an hour. You become awake. From the moment your eyes push open the doors to light, to the moment you rest them for the night, you are a stream of energy flowing through space. If you are always waiting for tomorrow, you are never going to know what today feels like. Don't let the harness of time restrict you from being free. Quantify your life on earth by the moments of how you think, and what you do. Be timeless.

"Absolute Happiness"

If you could escape reality, where would you go? Encapsulated within each one of us is the quest for happiness. To some, happiness is obtained easily while to others it comes at a brutal price. Many believe there's no amount of money that could purchase happiness, and very few think happiness comes from within. Not obtainable, not achievable, but rather an intrinsic overlaying force that stabilizes the mind. I'm sure you can relate to the common things that bring about joy. Such things like materialistic toys with a high sticker price or events that give you the bursting adrenaline rush to feel alive. This sunburst appearance of happiness is not a stable consistent form of homeostasis. This rising and falling of energy misleads you into a state of false security. The feeling, although exhilarating and stimulating in the moment, is all too short to be true happiness. You're rolling on the ground. Turning and twisting. Your skin feathers across the grass as you crawl towards the edge. You're lying on your back as your face panels towards the sun. Closer to the edge, you peek over. You rise to your feet and jump. You are in free fall. Gravity vacuums you quickly to earth, as you plummet with freedom to the ground. You're swimming. Deep below sea level you continue to drop. Plunging deeper and deeper, you're focused on the moment. The water compresses your lungs as you search for life. Time. Time is running out as your chest wall continues to deflate. This is the only true test of time. When your life depends on it, you become a victim of your fate and the only seconds that matter then are the ones granted to you in that solitary moment. This is happiness. It is these temporary, obsolete moments that can reinvigorate you and remind you what it means to be human. A human is not a robot, nor a slave. You are a free-thinking, free spirited entity sharing this planet with billions of other organisms. You must open your eyes and ears to your surroundings to capture the magnificence. As a human you are subjected to many biological and chemical processes occurring within you, and these processes all have trigger points associated with them. The earth around you contains all the stimulants necessary to activate your trigger points. You must expose yourself to the stimulants, yield to them, and allow them to penetrate deep within your cells to provide the most sensational of feelings: true happiness. To be in this constant euphoric state is to be blissfully mesmerized.

"A Sun's Vision"

The sun rose today before you did. In a life of inconsistency and chaos, you can find the rising and setting of the sun to be of most fascinating phenomenons. There should never be a time when your life's struggles exceed that of the big yellow circle above. It is omnipotent, giving light to life and life a vision, and without the sun we would all be blind. But, if you were blind, would you still need the sun? When you look out at an object, the light that is reflected from that object to your eye helps form an image of what you see. The blind, however, are not able to utilize the reflected light from objects to form images of what they see. But, that does not mean that a blinded person cannot see objects the same as you or I. The blinded do not depend on reflected light to form images in their heads of the objects in their surroundings because they can use their imagination. They use other stimulants to provoke trigger points in their brain to bring light to darkness. For instance, the blinded can use detailed descriptions from others or the topography engraved in touch to help the imagination create the world around them. In this way, the most imaginative people on earth are those that can't see, for their perspective on their external environment relies on the images they create inside of their head. Close your eyes, take two deep, elongated peaceful breaths. Lift your hands up. You are floating, high above the clouds you drift above the rest of the world. The wind blows through your arms as you continue to evaporate into space. Now you are back on earth. You walk up to the nearest tree and close and once again close your eyes. You wrap your arms around the tree like it was the first time hugging your first teddy bear. What do you see? Perhaps, a bulky, monstrous, hard-shelled, corrugated object sticking out of the ground. Or maybe something else. But it's a tree you are told. But you've never seen a tree before. So what do you see? This the power of self-imagery and it give's light to life and life a whole new meaning. Ultimately, given other external cues like sound, touch, smell, you may too be able to form the world around you in the image of creativity. This extraordinary phenomenon demonstrates that you can perceive the world around you in a way that is completely unique to you. Go out into the world like the blind man, and use your imagination to create a world you love.

"The Balance of Life"

Every second that goes by is another second closer to the end of your life. We weren't chemically engineered to last forever. We're mortal beings in an immortal world. Life is all around us. Nature is the true time of life, and the plants and animals that surround you are the engines of the world. We are only periphery end users in this game of nature. Honor the life around you, for it holds the true secrets of happiness. Walk outside and observe what you see and you will find yourself utterly intrigued by the extreme amount of natural consistency that takes place around you. The bird flies across the blue sky on a sunny day. The ant scavenges across tiny cracks and crevices to find its way. The bee hums its way from one flower to the next. And this happens, along with millions of other processes, day in and day out, around the clock, constantly and spontaneously. As highly evolved superior organisms we feel entitled to the world around us. We take for granted the simple things in life and we elect to ignore these minute natural processes. Why don't we walk outside each day with the objective to search and discover? Today, go out as an activist for earth and focus on your surroundings. Open your eyes, bend your ears, and engage in your internal and external audiences. Then, possibly, you can establish relationships with those audiences. A relationship exists when two separate entities establish common ground between one another. Communication doesn't require exchanging words. Rather, communication can be more silent in the form of simple subtle acknowledgment of each other's presence. So when you walk outside today and see the bee buzz by you, acknowledge its presence, respect its abilities of life for it has qualities that you do not possess, i.e. flying. Nature provides the best platform for your creative potential. Recognize the gifts of others and you will be able to unfold the beauty of the world around you. Yes you may be able to end that bee's life by swatting it against the wall with the local newspaper. But that would not be respecting that organism for the life it possesses and the gifts that it brings to the world and your surroundings. As humans, we have the ability to destroy, but this ability is more of a weakness than anything. The act of killing does not favor growth and progression. Killing is a diminishing act that results in the reduction of something beautiful. Excess and the control of excess differ from the irreversible act of reduction. You can control your eating habits and become healthier but that is a reversible act if you chose the next day to overconsume. Irreversibly extracting your tooth, however, gives you one less tooth to function with. The same principles apply to your life and so by killing other organisms like the bee you limit your ability to appreciate all the gifts of nature. You must establish relationships with all living organisms. By the simple acknowledgement of one beings existence and respect for that organism's life, you can recognize powers of nature that are beyond even your own imagination.

"One Second Later"

It only takes a second to realize that everything in your life has changed. 3600 seconds in a day, 365 days in a year, and just within one second's time your life can be altered forever. Life happens in cycles, history repeats itself, and we all procure the same repetitive motions and behaviors that keep us alive. Eat, drink, sleep! Pretending to exist in a life that we call our own, when in reality, we are just living in a loophole of someone else's vision for the world. Today is not tomorrow and tomorrow is not today, so live in the moment, for it only takes one second for your tomorrow to be changed forever. A meal tastes best straight out of the oven. So too is a moment only as good as the second it occurs in real time. Thus, capture each moment for the time it unfolds in front of you. Integrate with it. Do not wait for the next time around, because planning causes you to forget the feeling of "now". The "now" feeling can only be felt if you are experiencing the experience. Do not step from one second to the next. Become the second of life that takes you from one place to the next. If your mind is worried about the future or reflecting on the past, then the "now" experience gets buried beneath a scrambled pile of disrupted thoughts and emotions. Forget yesterday, ignore tomorrow, and live now. That one second that can change your life forever can only happen if it occurs in a moment that catches you off guard. The mind has the ability to anticipate all events; you just need to allow your mind to focus on the second that could change your life forever.

"Out of the Box"

Do you ever sit and wish you could escape the curse of the four walls. They follow you wherever you go and shun the light of the world from entering your life. They provide a false sense of security for your happiness and comfort. Each day, without hesitation, you travel from one 90-degree room to the next. Strip down the 4 walls of your false sense of comfort and live outside of your box. Our life becomes a momentary representation of the room we are confined to. It's a space, designed by another human being with the intent that it will contain you, just as a box is engineered to contain a certain amount of items. The more you live within the 4 walls of life, the more you become an item in a box. The earth is spherical, 360 degrees in circumference and yet we still choose to confine ourselves to the 90 degrees that form two adjacent walls. Live outside those 4 walls. Do not let your mind be satisfied with the life someone else created for you within those walls. Wake up in a room, eat in the kitchen room, jump in your confining car, go to work and sit in a chair inside of a designated space or room. This is your life! It wasn't designed for you to be free, feel free, or express yourself freely. No, it was designed to contain you, like an item in a box restricted to a certain amount of space and range of mobility. Expand your life beyond it and you shall find comfort in the spherical nature within earth's true form. There is no end to your desires. What awaits you is a continuous path of potential encircling you each and every day. You must think bigger than the rooms you choose to live in. Escape to the outdoors, get to know the life beyond the box and you shall seek freedom in expression in all that you do. The next time you look out at the world, observe the people around you and you will see people content in their ways and content in their confined space of nature. Open the curtain and jump out and into the open bliss. Push outward and onward until the walls around you collapse and you can run free. To be robotic is to be programmed to limitations. But to be human is to explore outside the boundaries of the box. It is only human nature to seek the path of least resistance, and staying within the boundaries certainly keeps life simple and controlled. But I challenge you all! Make the world your box and you shall see the greater glories of life. You shall see what no other person sees. This world is full of hidden secrets and pleasantries that provide all the beauty and happiness one human can ever dream of, but what separates you from it is your box so escape it today and forever be free from imprisonment within your own world of restrictions.

"The Illusion of a Friend"

There are times you find yourself so caught up around the daily rush that you forget those most important in your life. Like just about anything, you get out what you put in. Relationships are no different and successful ones require work. To call someone your friend is to assign them some title, an ambiguous designation that they don't deserve. A friend is a brother/sister, a lover/partner, an umbrella/safety net, and most importantly there for you no matter what. A friend is the one that does anything for you, anytime and anywhere. To be a friend is not earning a degree on someone's wall of life. It's not leveling up in some video game. Being a friend means to be selfless and accepting. A friend captures the worst times and the best, and knows just how to bring out the best in you. In every sense of the word, our friends are omniscient. Their all-knowing powers provide us with limitless solace. And yet, beyond all the qualities a friend takes on lies just one most important: trust. We all have secrets, we all have problems and it's the outsourcing of those problems and secrets upon our friends that makes them omnipotent. Without relinquishing the rights to your most dark thoughts and experiences, you would have nothing but an empty vessel inside of you. This empty vessel would house all of your suppressed memories of life, and would lock them there forever providing them the dark nourishment to impact your thoughts on a daily basis. These dark thoughts attached to the dark alias we call our secrets is just an excuse for privacy, and an unhealthy one at best. Use your friends as outlets for the deep dark secrets that lie within. To outburst them onto your friends is an act of liberation. We all go through life with secrets. Some more dangerous than others, while most are more damaging than not. A secret is a lie, and if you hold them to yourself on a constant basis then you will be lying to yourself on a constant basis. Openness is the only true key to happiness, and to be open with yourself and those around you is to be real with yourself and those around you. No one enjoys an alias, a temporary. We all want the real thing. The only secret you should have in life is the one you don't know you possess. Let the world see you for your greatest gifts and you shall see no secret untold. The only true secret within you should be the potential for greatness you have in life. Find a friend. Do not let them go. And show them that true happiness is best obtained when shared.

"Not The Last Day"

So you wake up one day, it's a normal day just like all the others. You have your breakfast, listen to your favorite morning tune, reflect on the day ahead, and then off to work you go. You're walking through the glass sliding doors to your workplace, drenched with optimism to start off the morning strong, and you look up and see a coworker rapidly approaching. You see the coworker perch his eyes towards you as he continues in your direction and so you stop to quickly realize you don't know him that well. In fact, the only common ground between the two of you is your occupation and place of work. The initial all-too familiar head-nod quickly transgresses into a face to face moment. You politely offer your most template of greeting expressions and he does the same. But what comes next, you could have never prepared for, especially not on a day filled with enthusiasm and zest for life. Your coworker poises his head, depresses his muscles of facial expressions, and with the faintest tone states "my brother just passed away last week". Death! What is it about death that makes the topic annoyingly awkward? We all know that death exists in the world but when it confronts us at our front door we can't help but wait for the moment it leaves. It's a part of everyday life, and a natural part of being human and mortal, but when it crosses our footpath we do everything possible to brush it to the side as quickly as we can. When someone brings up death, we're so uncomfortable to the point where no one knows what to say or how to say it. Most people, plain and simple, feel better just ignoring it or trying to change the subject as quickly as possible. As humans, we fear death so much that it's the least discussed topic in the human literature. However, it's time you take ownership of this normal process of life. It is, and will always be, a part of being human and you need to learn how to express yourself even in the context of death. It's hard to find the good in death, especially when nothing good comes out of it. However, death offers us something that most people lack in about 99.9% of their life: reflection. Death gives us the much needed opportunity to take a back seat and reflect on an individual and the life they lived. Death yields the unique opportunity to identify one's accomplishments and value in the world, and to elucidate what it was that made that individual special. Their characteristics, demeanor, successes, and their strengths and weaknesses all play a part in the equation. It's the moment you can really sit back and reflect on what that person contributed to themselves and others during their life. You may find it ironically humorous that it takes termination to bring about such illumination, and that we should really learn to compliment people for what they do in life while they are physically present to enjoy it. Learn to make others feel appreciated for what they do while they are alive to feel the reward. Why wait until a time when that person isn't present to enjoy the fruitful expressions of your paid compliments and accolades? If you must help someone get over someone that has passed then do it in a very positive way. The best commiseration of the dead revolves around stimulating those people mourning the dead into thinking about what it was for that person to be alive. You must probe into the history of the deceased. I call it "fatal distraction of the living". Ask your coworker things such as "what was his/her name?" or "What did your brother like to do the most?" Then tell the person mourning over the dead to go out and do that certain action in honor of the deceased individual. Go out and do what the person that died loved to do, in honor of him/her. This is a way to preserve the deceased individual's favorite moments in life. And in some ways, you can absorb that person's qualities and spirits of character by acting them out yourself or directing others to do the same. The energy lost from one then can be transferred to you or another in the form of active revitalization of that person's skills and interests. You must approach each day as an opportunity to make others proud of their personal traits. Pay compliments to everyone you know and let the sweet fruits of your efforts spread their flavor around the world.

"The Supreme Natural Interface"

You look out at the ocean and see an endless time as far as the eye can see. The sky is painted with a deep royal blue that wraps its arms around you like a warm blanket on a cold winter morning. The clouds interlace the sky like a powdery backsplash upon a starry night. The ocean crumbles beneath the sky like a never ending somersault, eventually unfolding upon the beach ahead. The vigilant seagulls flood the skies above like crackling background noise. The sun stands tall as a glowing watchtower looking down upon you. These are the interfaces of life. They are amongst you at all times and you just need the visual clarity to see them. When you step outside and observe the world around you, try to discover these surrounding interfaces. Your environment is simply the culmination of these intertwining portraits of nature. However, these portraits can fall under two realms of existence: man-made or natural. It's the natural portraits that come together in the most synergistic of fashions, whereas the man-made interfaces that surround you will seem forced and interrupted. The most pleasurable sites in the world derive their beauty from the natural interfaces that outline them. With your toes in the sand, you can feel the earth shifting below. This is the interface between the human and natural phenomenons. This is the ultimate interface that you can experience. On the other hand, the ultimate interface that you can observe lies strictly within the natural boundaries of life. The only way to interact with nature is by integrating with it. Dip your feet into the sand; let the tiny granules tussle between your toes as you embrace the cleansing action that it brings. Stretch your body across the beach platform and let the sun rays ionize your skin to give it the energy it needs to start the day off right. You are one with nature once you become one with its components. To simply exist amongst the surface is to be a bystander amongst the game of life. Get your hands dirty, kick the ball around once or twice, and let the natural arena around you show you how to play the game. As human beings, we not only have the desire to interact with our surroundings, but also possess the ability to change them. The ultimate natural interfaces cannot be changed, for they are impenetrable to human influence. This is the beauty of these interfaces for they possess the superior power to resist human interaction. The breaching of ocean waves upon the beach, the rising and setting of the sun are interfaces of nature that cannot be changed, and therefore are supreme. Imprinting your hand upon the sand has its limits and the sign you create cannot be undone. Like a sandy beach on a sunny day you must find that natural interface that speaks to you. You must find that interface that is unchangeable, and so that it becomes a place for you to grip it vigorously to take control of your surroundings. And so then in that moment, you can integrate with the interface only through your imagination. In the supreme natural interface, you cannot concretely change the physical constants. You will only be able to use your imagination to abstractly change the physical constants within a certain supreme natural interface. You're sitting outside on a warm summer evening. The sun is setting to your west side and as you look up you see a dull cluster of dark clouds drifting toward you. You stop. This is a supreme natural interface. You close your eyes, leap toward the skies and with the faintest whistle, blow the clouds away. Once you've implemented your creativity into the sound and structure of your supreme natural interface, you can then move to integrate within it. By integrating with it, you can then escape your reality. You must come to accept that there are these differences in our perceived environments, and that acknowledging these differences allows you determine what you can and cannot control. We all strive to be in control as we search for ways to be in the driver seat of our surroundings. But in life, you must learn to be the passenger to your surroundings so that you can use your mind to become the driver. But only through the passenger's eyes can you visualize what's truly around you and experience it. The next time you sit on a beach; do so with a passenger's perspective. You will find yourself more in control of what you don't know then in control of what you do know. You see, you listen, you integrate, and then you submit your thoughts to the creative desires of your imagination. You let your abstract thoughts dominate your reality so that the imagination becomes the reality amidst the supreme natural interface. The only choice you have is the selection of your surroundings. Once the selection process takes place you then can proceed with the integration process which begins as a concrete passenger and ends as an abstract driver. Then and only then, can you change the supreme natural interface to be your own break from reality.

The 3 Modes of "YOU" and "I"

You look out at the world in search for a deeper meaning and instead stumble upon others in search of the same thing. Each human has the innate quest for their vocational purpose in life, and yet most of us will fall short of it. Look out at the world and seek refuge within the miles of land beyond you and embrace its purpose to provide insight into your greater path. Carving into this land is not simple for it requires a sharp mind and a trailblazing motive. This land does not come with an instruction manual. The only rule of the land before you is that it is present. Whether you choose to walk straight, jump, or stand still is a decision you will make each day when you enter the world with a vision. The hope is for this vastness of space to be equally shared by all of us. You start by claiming a very tiny portion for yourself, defined by the surface area of your own two feet and the vertical volume occupied by your body. This is your space. It's a strict volume of space virtually granted to each and every one of us. There's a law in physics that states no two things can occupy the same space at the same time. So why fight over it? Enjoy the volume of air and surface area of land granted to you by your physiologic existence, and be content with it. There is so much hostility in the world over space and for absolutely no reason when you consider the fact that the entire planet Earth contains more volume of space than any aggregation of organisms could ever possibly occupy. Instead, we should all just concern ourselves with our own center of locus called "I". This is the only space "I" can truly occupy at one given moment in time and as such remains the only space that "I" needs to worry about. You can look out at people and retrieve confusion in the midst of stability. People have no idea of their purpose in life and yet the world continues to function coherently. Essentially, most of us are placated into thinking we are fulfilling our purpose. If every human stopped for just one second, took a brief moment in time to expel their mind from the false reality they've created and would recalibrate their thoughts toward greater purpose, then the world would be in pandemonium. I know not what I do for I know not who I am. These are the words of pandemonium. We are all standing on a false platform of stability in the form of our job, our duties, and ultimately our life. At times you may mistake this platform of stability for happiness, but beneath this platform is a foundation of chaos banging at the door trying to get you to see the light. But the only light you can see is the one that comes in the form of a 60 watt light bulb, the light created by humans to make you believe you have the power of light at your grasp at all times. However, the only true light is through the sun, and it rises every morning to touch all the lands' of the earth. This is the true light, the true owner of the land amongst us all. Can you see the light? As humans we enjoy learning, creating goals, and bettering ourselves. But these qualities are all empty unless you attach them to your true vocation. Living atop the false platform of stability will only continue to put your mind in a constant flux of instability. It's equivalent to condemning yourself to a solo raft adrift at sea with no land in sight. We all need to jump off our rafts and start swimming to our destiny. Call this salvation, call this hopefulness of a better life, or just call it absolute happiness. When you look out at people, you see the physical formula of an individual that contains an internal entity belonging strictly to them. Fortunately, you also possess this internal entity denoted as "you". This is your thoughts, your mind, and your subconscious that you alone possess. There's no key to this door within you, and the only one that can open this door is you. Most of us safeguard our "you" and overprotect our "I". The "you" contains a past, a present, and a future and our mind is constantly battling between these three segments. We're always reflecting on our past, neglecting the present, and fearing the future. It's a phenomenon that allows us to possess a "you" that is partitioned between 3 modes at all times. However, we can only physically exist in one of these modes: the present. This is the infinite flux of our internal entity. We substitute between these 3 partitioned modes to help cope with the present. If the present defines the mode, and you are in the past, does that mean someone else is living in your future? The next time you look out at someone, seize the moment, and imagine which mode they're in. Each new day gives you the opportunity to become more in tune with your "you" and the freedom to use your "I" to make a difference.

"A Breath of Happiness"

Life isn't always so easy. Sometimes you need to forget the problems and escape from the adversity you face. Sometimes you need to leave your life behind and start up a new one. We can't always have the things that we want because most things that we want require achievement. If everyone just got everything they wanted in life, then people would lose their motivation to try and achieve new things. We all search for the things that we don't have, but yet we all end up acquiring the things that we don't really want. So it becomes a balancing game between trying to maximize the things you want and reducing the things you don't need. If the curve shifts to either side of that balancing act, you will start to feel dissatisfied with your life. There are people everywhere in search of something. And it's that constant search for something that will keep you from achieving nothing. To achieve you need to forget that you ever wanted something and work as if you're in need of nothing. This will allow you to focus on what it is that you really need in life as opposed to putting all of your energy and focus into trying to just achieve new things. If you focus too hard on just trying to achieve, you start to lose sense of what it is you are actually trying to accomplish. So, what is it in life that you absolutely need? There's no amount of anything concrete that can make you happy. The happiness you achieve within yourself comes from an abstract realization in the form of reflection. True tranquility is only obtained when the mind realizes it need's nothing. When you acquire something new in life, you instantly get excited because you feel a sense of betterment. But, if the things that made you happy actually mad you eternally happy then you would no longer search for something additional. It's not about the possession of that new item that will make you happy but rather your mind's interpretation of happiness associated with procuring that item that will make you happy. We all want to be happy. We all want to better ourselves, but we remain slaves to materialistic handcuffs strapped around our minds. The only things you actually need in life are those that are free to us all: the air in your lungs and the natural elements on earth. These are the true gifts of happiness. The next time you walk outside, just pause for a moment and take a deep breath. Feel the power associated with the air that fills your lungs and expands your body. This is the breath of happiness. You are bringing into your body the sources of life and, with each breath, giving yourself the chance to enjoy it.

"Problems are Fictitious"

People tend to look towards others to solve their problems, when mostly they need only to look within themselves. There is not a single person in this world that doesn't encounter problems. Take each problem as an opportunity to change the way you think. The problem gives you the opportunity to identify your liabilities in life. These liabilities can come in all different forms: vulnerabilities, ineptitude, weakness, or simply just voids. By first identifying the type of problem that exists you can then successfully create a solution. If it's a vulnerability that haunts you, then you most likely suffer from an emotional complex. The simple solution being to associate each negative thought you may develop with a positive thought and then in time all of your pessimism will be converted to optimism. If it's ineptitude that's causing you problematic distress, then stop worrying about how bad you are at it and start working at becoming better.

Become adept at the inept. If it's a weakness that you possess and cannot control, then find ways to become stronger. Perhaps you have no self-discipline and can't control your urges in life. In this case, you must first identify the urge or the temptation, and then start by changing your environment to a context that does not contain those urges. For instance, if your weakness involves indulging in your sweet tooth, then when you go shopping, skip the ice cream isle. If your weakness is alcohol, then find yourself entertainment at the local bingo club on Friday nights instead. Now, most of us associate our problems with our voids. We all desire that which we feel we lack. We want what our neighbor has, or what the movie stars and high profile public figures possess. These voids stem out of jealousy. Find yourself amongst people that envy you for what you have and you will no longer feel deprived of what you don't have. Some people have more problems than others, but what brings us all together is that we all have at least one problem in each of the following categories: vulnerabilities, ineptitude, weakness, or voids. You must identify the problem or problems within each one of these categories and work each day to depress them behind a curtain of progress.

"Mind and Emotion"

The mind is such a powerful device that if used improperly can cause massive destruction of the self. What separates your mind from the next person's mind is the power of experience. Each one of us has experiences, some more unique than others, but all of which have inflicted modifications on our "self". There are two main ways to live life: proactively or reactively. Living proactively means to use the mind to anticipate future events and then to adjust the physical self to such anticipated events. To live your life reactively means to let your mind process incoming events on a second by second basis and then to let your mind determine your next pursuit of action. If you have a high emotional intelligence, then you live life reactively and your mind remains in constant control of your surroundings. Essentially, you live life through this window of mental control that is tinted for your comfort and security. It's through this mental tinted wall that you create around yourself, that keeps you in a controlled environment, separated from the spontaneity of life. This type of high emotional intelligence individual would not prefer to see a new flower blossom. Instead, they'd rather see a blossomed flower that they've already seen before. The mind is such a powerful machine that it can actually regulate the physical body's spontaneous nature, keeping it confined within certain parameters. If you're living inside of your head, living inside of your own deep mental thought, then you're not actually living at all. You're living within a certain frequency of neuronal transmission, dictated by central and peripheral nervous center stimuli. No more than what an idle computer on standby would be like. You're not living by the laws of entropy provided to us all in the form of liberty and free will. This mental imprisonment is what prevents you from quitting your job in search of a new one, or from going on that vacation that you've always imagined. These mental handcuffs restrict you to a certain limited range of motion and way of life that overtime condemns you to the wheelchairs of a handicapped existence. Essentially, you're living in a body where your emotions are glued to your feet. Whatever past experiences forced your mind into this confined box, they've caused you to essentially stop living as an autonomous being. Instead, you have allowed your mind to set the rules of how much freedom you will have. If everyone were etched in a stand-by mode of an existence, then nothing would ever get accomplished. You need to shut down the computer, re-boot and resynchronize your mental hard drive with a new type of mental software so that your new set of programs and principles give you the complete liberty to explore the world around you.

The Thought Medium"

What is everyone around you thinking about? Look to your left and you will see a person that is dressed like you, has the same basic anatomical phenotype as you, but yet sits with different thoughts than you. Look to your right and you will see a different person, once again who looks like you, and who wears a pair of shoes like you, but yet still someone who possesses an entirely different spectrum of thoughts than you. You listen to the voices inside of your head and you can't help but wonder if they are your thoughts or the thoughts of those next to you right now. Is it possible that your thoughts are being manipulated by the thoughts of others close to you? If the atmosphere is the ultimate medium for the transmission of bacteria, viruses, sound waves, electrical waves, than it should be true that this same medium of the atmosphere should be able to conduct and transmit the waves of human thought. There are certain thoughts that enter your mind more frequently than others. These thoughts have a commonality amongst all people and thus present at a higher rate within the atmospheric medium. Thoughts such as, "what am I doing right now?", or "is this really all there is too life?", or "when am I going to eat next?" may seem common enough. The thoughts themselves are not as important as the frequency at which you generate them. Putting emphasis on certain queries within your life assigns those ideas a higher thought medium factor. Open your mind to the voices of your neighbors, and you shall receive the knowledge and wisdom of those around you. Profess your thoughts with subtleness and you will see them penetrate others with greater purpose. In this way, your thoughts can be transcribed across a medium that influences those around you. The next time you find yourself talking inside of your head, stop for a moment, and reflect what it is your mind is trying to tell you. Talking to yourself is your mind's internal safety mechanism for reflection. The mind knows when it needs to pause and just take a deep breath. So take a deep breath and let the mind intake a fresh flow of thoughts and ideas. Reflection is a healthy part of life because just like sleeping it provides us with the necessary decompression and rebooting that our brains require in order to be a in a healthy balanced state. Your goal is to establish an external and internal homeostasis with your surroundings. Be relaxed, find solace in others, and pursue each day like it was the first day to the rest of your life. The balanced nature of all organisms comes with it the waxing and waning of successes and failures. Nevertheless, the laws of equilibrium can be applied to our thought processes in the formula of incoming thoughts + information = reflection + internal thoughts. I know not who I am for I know not what I do. If you want to exchange your thoughts with the person next to you, then you must visualize yourself inside of his/her head.

"Risk Finds The Reward"

There's such a risk associated with living your life that you often wonder of a world where risk didn't exist at all. You find commonly in others that risk evaluation is a big part of their daily decision making. But why should risk be a factor of life at all? If you're actually experiencing your life to the fullest, then risk should never be part of the equation. Instead, balancing the left from the right begins with the initiation of a thought inside of your mind and ends with an afterthought. If an idea, a concept, a goal, or a challenge enters your mind it means that your brain has responded to some external stimulus within the world around you and that external stimulus has provoked the deepest centers of your brain to recognize that stimulus as important. And if this stimulus is significant enough to provoke such thoughts of curiosity within you, then it probably means this stimulus is interesting to you, and therefore the pursuit of this fascinating stimulus should never be considered risky but rather just simply living. It's Saturday morning, and for the first day this week you awake with complete ownership of the day ahead. No alarm clock sergeant buzzing you into work. No obligations or sense of urgency souring your morning routine. Instead, a peaceful early bird chirping welcoming you to the morning sunrise. A fresh breath of happiness and the day is yours. You decide to throw on some gym clothes and jump on your bike. You start riding and slowly lose yourself in reflective thought. Minutes go by and when you come through, you realize you are nowhere close to home. You've wandered off to a strange and unfamiliar place, but you keep going. You are lost. You decide to investigate the unknown territory, and you do it without caution. Deep into the woods you travel with no one to tell you otherwise. You find a path, unlike any other path, that you decide to head down. A path connected to many other paths. It goes up and it goes down and stretches as far as the eye can see. Your destiny awaits you. To say you're going to take a risk on something is merely to say that you're living your life. Being risky simply means you're deviating from a standard path of life and the risk you take is governed by comparisons, relativity, and predictive outcomes. But deviation from a normal path should never be considered risky; it should only delineate differences in choices and decision making. When you head to the local mall to purchase a brand new outfit, you may often find yourself lost within a plethora of choices. Grappling over this outfit versus that outfit, you may spend hours inside of a mall trying to make the best choice. In the end, you purchase something that you've decided best suits you. You don't buy clothes for yourself with the thought that they would look perfectly on someone else. You buy clothes specifically for you because you like them. Typically, you have no problems walking out of that mall wearing an outfit completely different from the person next to you. Why should taking risks to live your life be any different? When making decisions you must make the decision because it best suits you, just as your outfit does. Don't make your decisions based on how others made their decision because in the end we all look different even in the same outfit. If a thought comes into your head that involves doing something, then just go and do it. No one ever accomplished anything great by evaluating their pursuit. They just did.

"The Progression of a Thought"

Look out around you and you will see others walking through life in a capsule of their own suppressed thoughts. You interact with them as they do with you, but together you both are just interacting within a protective barrier of appropriateness. This happens when you say something to someone but actually mean something else. Your mind is designed to contain your thoughts alone. What you feel and think is preserved land, unoccupied by anyone else. When you communicate with another person you are showing them your land, but deep down you always know that there is a fence up separating you from them. The only true way to progress is to innovate and the only way to innovate is by observing the missing links within the world around you. Once you open your eyes to your surroundings you can mentally critique your perception of things: "I like the color of that building, or "that sidewalk is awfully decrepit", or "I like the way that bird can just fly above me without any restrictions but those set by its own wings". These are "analyzing thoughts" that we generate based off our observations of our surroundings. With every "analyzing thought" comes with it an "improvement thought". The "improvement thought" is what we subject our creative imagination to and is the arena of thinking outside of the box to try and make things you see in the world better. The goal and secret to innovation is to dwell in the moment of an "improvement thought". And the only way to capture the beauty and potential of an "improvement thought" and bring it to surface is by pausing to reflect on a certain "analytical thought". Then, each "after thought" derived from the "analytical thought" will serve as a supplemental "progressive thought" to the desired "improvement thought". For example, if you walk outside and see it is raining, your initial "analytical thought" might be "it is raining and I don't want to get wet". The goal is to dwell on this "analytical thought" so that you can develop creative after-thoughts like "rain hits the top of my head and ruins my hair" or "when water gets on my face it causes me to itch". By focusing on the after-thoughts you then start to think of progressive thoughts like "if I put something above my head it will stop the rain". This is your innovative moment. Instead of deciding to run to your car whereby you would be met with a series of new "analytical thoughts", you focus on the "improvement thought" to drive your innovation behind the original "analytical thought". Analyze the world for what you see in front of you, be there for that moment, and your surroundings will illuminate the answers to all of your problems. Be vigilant each day, so that you are able to open up your umbrella upon each challenge you face.

"Relationships Give and Take"

There comes a time in your life, when you will enter a relationship of some form or another. This relationship may be with another person, mate or friend, an animal such as the domesticated beloved family dog or cat, a spiritual entity, or perhaps more simply with yourself. And so, the form of relationship that you take on is not so as significant as the approach that you follow. Interestingly, the nature of any relationship adheres to the same set of principles. However, distilling out the main components of any relationship is certainly not easy, and in fact can be quite tantalizing considering no two relationships are the same. The major factor guiding any relationship is the dynamic element of "consistency". You strive each day to make that day easier than the previous. You do this by finding shortcuts in your routine, by investigating the things you don't fully understand, and by finding ways to simplify your life. You do this because you must in order to survive. Information and behavioral consolidation is common to all humans because it allows us time to reprogram our routines so that we don't become too overwhelmed. With consistency comes familiarity and with familiarity comes complacency. Typically, a relationship will change as the members of that relationship change. As we move through time and life, we uncover the hidden secrets of our future. We adapt better to our habitat and acquire new skills to manipulate our world to be in favor of making our life more consistent. You must recognize and be mindful that as you change, so will your relationships with family, friends, pets, friends, and most importantly yourself. All relationships are dynamic and by neglecting this dynamic nature you instigate a downturn spin on the relationship. Each relationship you have should be treated like a sports game. There are offensive players, which are aggressive and active, and there are defensive players, which are more passive. The only way any relationship will ever work is if both members play the same position and work as a team within that position. If one member plays offense while the other plays defense, the relationship will eventually develop discourse simply because the two members on the team will not be on the same page. By playing the same position in a relationship, you can identify with and share similar responsibilities. And do not try to play every position in life, for it will lead you to have the ball in your hands at all times. And this will cause your life to be saturated with stress and responsibility. If you are ever involved in a committed relationship and would like to put your best foot forward in hoping to achieve longevity then you need to play the same position. The bottom line is new shoes will always look good in the window, but it's the old ones that ultimately feel most comfortable. Also, the menu of life has a lot of different options to offer you, but the dish we enjoy most is the one we are most familiar with. Find a partner in life that compliments you in mind and body and together you may retrieve all the knowledge and strength to combat any challenge.

"Inside The Animal's Mind"

Sit down today and think about what other organisms in the world might also be doing at this very moment. Look inside your brain and turn toward an imagination filled with conceptual images of things that are familiar to you. These images are in the form of animals, trees, and flowing rivers. These are the natural forces of life that drive the world's ecosystems. As an outsider you can only but wonder if these organisms possess thought as you do. Are they viewing the world we live in with an objective eye or do they just exist as background energy beings? The moose that travels the dense forest is structurally amplified but simple in function. The human, on the other hand, possesses a complex function within a simplified exoskeleton. The human physical abilities are complex in nature but minute in size. Size does not directly correspond to function, but function directly parallels complexity. Humans have superior complexity compared to the fellow moose, but the moose possesses greater size. The bumble bee, in turn is small, but yet plays a colossal role in nature's yearly revitalization cycle. Evolution has a place for all of us in its grand design, and it's the process of natural selection that makes each organism in the world today unique to its time. Each living organism possesses a unique ability. If you want to discover an organism's unique ability, you must put yourself in that organism's mind and acquire its thoughts. The moose navigates the forest with little fear. Its large size makes it resistant to many smaller predators, but yet it still remains a source of prey in nature's game. The moose wanders the forest with an idle mind. It doesn't think about what it is eating, it just eats. When it walks it thinks about the path of least resistance. You, on the other hand, walk with eagerness towards greater purpose, but with an idle mind you can too live the life of a moose. The human might turn right because it provides an opportunity for more peaceful scenery. The moose will inevitably turn left because it senses the quickest route to food, shelter, or water. Think with purpose and function and identify with the gifts of nature for when you simplify the things around you, the walk becomes smooth and straight.

"Mental Branding"

The most incomplete thought is the one preceded by the current thought. In life, we jump from one incomplete thought to the next and eventually arrive at a singular idea. An idea is not necessarily a collective assimilation of thoughts but rather just a concise establishment of one singular thought. You must harness the inner potential of an incomplete thought to arrive at your subconscious understanding of the world around you. Instead of jumping from one place to the next, pause and let your mind freeze itself in a singular moment in time. You are in the shower. Water is gushing out of the nozzle, suspended above you, like a busted fire hydrant. As the water rapidly falls, it quickly meets its buffered destination upon your skin. The water sprinkles down your body and cleanses your skin in a delicate fashion. The shower is your safe-haven. We all have that place in our life where we feel absolute comfort and peace. For some it might be their car, while for others it could be their walk to work. Nonetheless, we all, over time, establish a safe-haven where we can escape the world and be alone with our own thoughts. It is during these times, within the comfort of your own designated personal space, that you generate deep reflection on the "self". And, it is during this time that you offer your deepest criticisms to the "self" and the things around you. The next time you are in the shower. Look around. You will see a plethora of different brand-name products joining your company. Each one associated with a unique description, slogan, and purpose. Grab the shampoo, surrender your belief into the product's claims, and lavishly indulge your hair with its contents.

You've done it. Your hair is now cleaner and stronger than before. Or is it? In life, you place a lot of trust in the information that is given to you. The shampoo product claims it will strengthen your hair, but if you refrain from using it, would you feel like your hair was deprived of strength? Now look around the rest of the shower and you will see 10 other products all claiming something you need that you really don't, Look more around your world and you will see thousands of products that you identify with each day that don't actually fulfill a role in your survival. The act of showering alone has a purpose to debride the body of noxious irritants and to provide cleansing action for good hygiene control. But one product after the next and you start to become one. Don't ruin the showering experience by deviating from its true purpose. Don't be a victim of the placebo effect. Be a creator of things and of yourself, and you find ways to use the world around you to make your story come alive.

"The Downhill Experience"

The downhill experience! Life would be so much easier if it were always downhill. One day, you jump out of bed and onto your bike. You hit the streets with your feet to both pedals, slowly building up enough energy to quickly move from one block to the next. You are only traveling at about 10mph, which is fast enough to feel like you are on a bike, but yet still slow enough to observe your peripheral surroundings. The biking experience is underway and you are feeling more liberated than ever before. Suddenly, you come to the top of a hill and look down. A straight path downhill confronts your eyes and you steamroll a mind of excitement. You position your front tire over the hill's breaking point and off you go. You are in a downhill motion. While moving downhill, you put the brakes on your body and let your mind absorb the kinetic energy of the downhill experience. You realize you don't have to expend any energy because the bike machine along with nature's laws of gravity is doing all the work for you. You are in a moment of momentum and the forces dictated by your body weight and speed set the tone for travel. While in this downward motion, look around and you will appreciate what it is that gives breath to freedom. It's the freedom of kinetic energy and it's the purest form of living that humans can achieve in the physical world. The human balance is dictated by an energy balance, and you need to maintain this balance in order to be in equilibrium. However, occasionally, your life curve shifts toward one end of the equation and you are no longer stable. Drugs, for example, cause you to shift your curve to the extreme highs of an unnatural state of mind. Roller coasters give you a similar high for it gives you the ability to free float in space without actually flying. The downhill experience is no different. It allows you to harness the kinetic energy that can liberate you positively. In life, this energy balance is a struggle for every human. Most of us go throughout our daily lives arrested by the potential energy of our efforts. We walk to work, we lift a box, we consume information, and we expend energy in routine, mundane ways. But you must find a way to channel that stored up energy into vehicles that can drive on any road. You must convert all of your potential energy to kinetic journeys to achieve ultimate freedom. At this point, you will no longer be bounded by your efforts, but instead will be a recipient of the free energy around you. Kinetic energy parallels the laws of entropy, which is why you should be encouraged to seek this free state of mind. Do not let your world and the people around you suppress your inner entropy and keep it bottled to a glass container that is corked. Go out and seek the kinetic energy that is granted to you each day. The more kinetic energy you take on, the more entropy you will encounter, and thus the more experiences you will have.

"The Power of Love"

The power of love is the only human endeavor one needs. To love another means to self-sacrifice your own needs and desires for those of another. When we reach out for love, we let our mind travel into a time and place where hate no longer exists. It's a lifestyle where giving becomes living. Give your heart to someone else and you shall see it work half as hard. So much of the human heart and mind is dedicated to things like competition, jealousy, greed, anxiety, and stress that we are over-working it. Liberate the heart from these stressors of life and fill it's chambers up with the power of love and you will find life to be much easier than before. If there was a recipe for love it would start with the ingredient of observation, continue on with identification, and then end with levitation. Look around your world, be the heart's bystander of weakness. There are many people around you that don't exercise the power of love within their heart. Identify these people and associate with them. Provoke them with your enthusiasm for life and challenge their poor outlook and negativity with rejoicing efforts of love. Find yourself amongst the cold hardened and pierce their hearts with the sword of love. Sometimes you're aiming for the bull's eye of life. You take a couple careful, calculated shots, hoping to hit your precise target. Most of those shots fall short, skew toward the left or right, but if you choose not to shoot at all, how will you expect to ever hit your target? Take your shots in life for each shot puts you within opportunity of your bull's eye. However, love doesn't have a bull's eye for love only works when the target least expects it. Love is the fuel to performing miracles in the world. You can't drive the car without the gas. You need love to find your way in the presence of those who need it too.

"Conscious Fixation"

There comes a time to just exist. To pause from the inanimate adversities of everyday life and let your mind escape all thought and query. It's the moment that you can freeze the time for a brief second and let your thoughts spill from your mind without any reservation. You take the cup of coffee next to you and drink it briskly. You find joy in the thought of disaster and chaos. You forget you have a name or that you belong to a specific gender or race. You just exist in the natural form of conscious thought, an imaginative state that lets you, simply, exist. This is a mental vegetative state. You're not exerting any physical energy, but yet your conscious mind is at work. In this state, your mind exits the body and essentially you have a mentally driven out-of- body experience. You forget everything around you exists, and you ignore all peripheral stimuli. You focus on nothing but the few thoughts that enter your mind and even then you find a way to quickly dismiss them. You don't want to think, you want no participation in analyzing the world around you and instead you want to be in a conscious state of wakefulness without actually having to do anything. This is a moment that not many people can obtain, especially in a society driven by the constant need for social and self-entertainment. Your brain enters this mode of conscious fixation as a rebellious act to the constant stimulation it receives daily. Sometimes your brain needs to just pause for a brief moment, decompress from its overloaded daily inputs, and then reboot itself. Most people satisfy this conscious fixation quota in the form of a consciously sedated REM sleep state. But some people are not granted the privilege to enjoy such ample sleep schedules and instead rely on conscious fixation. The moment when you completely ignore everything within you, of you, and around you, and you just exist. Now breathe. Your chest rises like smoke from a chimney. You ponder. You question. You find meaningless answers to the noise inside of your head. Black or White? Stop or Go? You take on another form of yourself. You're thin air slipping through all the cracks. Now breathe again. You're alive.

"The Others"

You sit outside and just wait. You're not in the action, but just a bystander of the world around you. It is upon this one moment that you decide to just sit back and observe. You focus intently on the periphery. By ignoring that which lies directly in front of you, and focusing on that which enters the lateral parts of your vision you become in tune to "the others". "The others" is an ambiguous denotation for those things in life that most people ignore on a daily basis. At the same time "the others" is 99.9% of what goes on around you. How could you focus on what's in front of you, without completely understanding the peripheral processes? In this sense, "the others" becomes more significant then what's directly in front of you. If you want to understand the problem you need to escape the problem and focus on the factors involved. There is so much to learn from what goes on along the outskirts of your life. Step outside the straight path you've carved for yourself up to this point and take your next step through an untouched path. This is where nature has been preserved and this is where great discoveries will occur. But, if you tread the path directly in front of you, then you shall soon find yourself at the end. Instead, reach beyond the path and there shall be no limits to your journey. There comes a time in life when reflection must extend from one's self and into the minds and behaviors of others, for as a growing species, comparative perspective yields the most predictable approach to improvement. By observing your neighbor take out the trash, you can comparatively decide a better way to take out your trash. This is how innovation is born, and you must break through the placenta of your direct vision to life and open your eyes for the first time to the world around you. Observe, analyze, and then improve upon the paths you see. We all have an agenda that we individually create and modify on a daily basis. Everyone's agenda is self-fulfilling and unique to their respective goals, and yet we all still find commonness in our ultimate societal views of how to live our life. Get a job, go grocery shopping, make phone calls, assume importance from the unimportant. These nuance motives are just distractions from the periphery. The true answer and beauty to life will always lie beside you. Just turn your head and you will find life staring you back right in the eye. All the answers to your problems lie hidden within the behaviors of "the others".

"Break the Mirror to Self-Reflection"

A natural part of being human involves the art of self-reflection; however, many people instead place too much honor in the need for physical reflection. Why do you feel the need to look into a mirror? When you look into the mirror, you are subjecting yourself to a level of criticism portrayed to you by others. You begin by looking at your own image through the eyes of others and you start to compare your physical display relative to the physical appearance of people you know. By looking in the mirror you already take a faulty first step toward self-detachment. The mirror is the worst channel for reflection. You stop being you and you start thinking in terms of a physical form that you believe others will most accept. This is the fallacy of the mirror and the dangers that lie within your physical reflection. The only healthy mirror is that which will give you insight into your mind's reflective thoughts. This is the true mirror of self-reflection and it only requires the simple act of closing your eyes and escaping into your mind's thoughts. The thought becomes the reflection of light that gives insight into the mental appearance of your mind. Instead of critiquing your blunders, you should let your mind ionize energy toward positive thoughts. And thus, thoughts such as "my skin looks pale", or "my hair could be longer" become thoughts of "how can I help someone today?" or "is there anything I can do to better myself?". In fact, the glass mirror you may look at each day will always be broken in some form or another. There's no such thing as perfection and when you look at your reflection in the mirror, you are only able to illuminate that which is wrong or misaligned. One is never satisfied with how they look so what positivity can they expect from the mirror act itself. So don't do it all? Break your mirror in life and tap into the reflection of your mind. The happiest people in life are those that neglect the significance of their physical appearance and instead allow others to focus on what it is inside of them that they have to offer the world: love, trust, happiness, joy.

"Finding the Edge"

The edge! This is the moment in life when you're balancing one extreme from the other. It's a distinct line between safety and chaos. If it were not for the edge, no one would understand boundaries. The edge maintains an unequivocal balance amongst all organisms of life and without it we would all just be in free-fall. There comes a time in your life when you realize that this edge exists, and that prior to your awareness of the edge, you were nothing more than a static object in life, like a cone. The ultimate decision to cross it, however, begs your innermost resistance to maintain the status quo of your life. The question then becomes whether you should live before, on, or over that edge. Those that confine themselves to the finite space before the edge are those people that calculate all the odds, make all the predictions, and succumb to all the anticipation of their life. They calculate all the risks but never acquire the audacity to function. They see the edge as a distant obstacle designed for an abstract place and time. Those that live on the edge represent a healthy balance between the extremists and the conservationists. They don't mind peering over the edge out of curiosity for what else lies beyond it, but they'll never actually be the ones to experience it. They question, they ponder, they imagine the feeling that would be associated with crossing the edge, but still remain adherent to the things they know best. And finally, you have those that cross the edge. They have no limits for their actions and see opportunity as an ability to experience life at the highest degree. They find the edge as an experience to be had, and the only way to experience it, is to cross it. The next time you find yourself at the edge, think twice about how you approach the experience. Standing on top of a rock at the edge of a cliff overlooking the vast ocean makes you feel on top of the world. At this moment you've forgotten your place in the world, and the only boundary in sight is the one created by the limits of your vision. And even this boundary can be crossed by the simple closure of your eyes and the opening of your mental vision in the form of your imagination. This boundary has no edge and the only edge then becomes the one beneath your two feet atop the cliff overlooking the ocean. Jumping is not an option, but flying is, and so you close your eyes, elevate your feet, and then jump. Your mind enters a rapid free-fall that breaks all the laws of gravity and you're moving at the speed of light. You're here, your there, you're everywhere and then you just stop. Stop high above the clouds, suspended there above the rest of the world, and you can finally open your eyes and see everything. You have no boundaries for at this point you lie above them. Nothing can control or limit your next move for the only thing left to do is fall. Fall deep into a state of liberation, for in your imagination your life is truly at your fingertips. You take your hands and lift up the sky to make room for your head as you lift it upward and stretch your legs out wide. Close your eyes to the vision of the imagination and into a dream state. The dreams are controlled by your physical and mental eyes and this becomes the ultimate experience on the edge. And then you can realize the truth: there is no edge.

"Your Weapon is Your Battle"

In the game of life we all have to choose our weapon. Based on our personalities, individual motives, and inherent energy continuum, we each represent a certain type of weapon. The internal guiding mechanism within each person is the weapon they possess. Some of us represent an assault rifle; rapid fire in nature. Those that bear this weapon are capable of multitasking beyond the average limits. They approach life in short bursts that, when amalgamated, form one strong bullet. Others may represent the shotgun, for its power and strength are derived from its patience. You wait for the big moment and then you attack in a glazing blow. And yet still others in life will possess a weapon, but will comfortably keep the safety lock in place. They prefer to not take any chances at all. They keep the entire weapon's power in an idle position. These members of society are in fact most fascinating, for their self-inhibiting position makes them most unknown. All of their potential becomes contained in the comforting state of the "safety lock", but at any given moment they could release it and become active in the game of life. The uncertainty associated with this type of passive position can make you unpredictable. This element of the unknown grants the highest potential for reward and thus you should seek to always maintain a "safety lock" position in your life. In fact, each person has a "safety lock" embedded within them to some degree. In life, some may be more active than others in one facet, while others are more active in another facet, but what is consistent amongst all of us is that we all hold back and maintain a "safety lock" position in one way or another or in one form or another. You are constantly changing, and within that act of change lies the secrets of your motivations. These motivations stem from the "safety lock", and by changing the position of your "safety lock" you can instigate your motivation to achieve things you never thought you could. Remember, you are a weapon, and through life you must discover what kind.

"Time Only Moves One Way"

Time! What we know about time is that all things in this world are associated with it. The clock is constantly ticking and as humans we are in a battle to fight against it. Some organisms in nature use time to their benefit whereas others use it destructively in a manner in which time becomes the center of everything they do. The simple question begs, is there really ever enough time? Everything you know, do, and achieve has a built in time component. Consider yourself arriving home from a day's work. You're mentally and physically submerged in fatigue and your stomach is stirring with the appetite for your favorite meal. You rush to the kitchen, kick open all the cabinets, and retrieve the ingredients to your favorite dish. Toppled with excitement, and eager to endorse an empty stomach, you realize one simple thing: this is going to take time. From the time it takes for certain ingredients to mix up properly to the time it takes for raw food to reach an edible temperature, you realize and understand that time is the limiting factor. This is your world as you know it because you are bounded by the perimeters of the small and big hands of life. The natural elements of life: hydrogen, oxygen, nitrogen, carbon are certainly essential, but above them all is time for without it nothing would progress. However, there comes a moment in your life when you must abolish the rules of time. You have a past, you live in the present, but you do not have a future that tomorrow guarantees. And so to approach life in a state of constant contention with time is to err on the face of limitation. If time is truly continuous, and thus infinite, then to live with the time and not for or by it, means you can also live forever. The next time you approach a task, express yourself in the moment of that time. Live with it, not for or by it. Time can only hurt you if you look at it from the wrong perspective. If you want to accomplish a task or a goal, never consider the amount of time it will take to achieve that task or goal, because then you might discourage yourself from pursuing it. Because time is finite you will never look at it from a perspective of abundance, and so instead you should just ignore it all together. You will never feel satisfied with the time you are granted. You will always want more. There's an hour left of work, it's a Friday, and you're sitting at your desk just counting down the minutes. You are no longer living, because the only thing you can think of is the moment when the clock strikes 5 and you are free to leave work and pursue all of the things you've pondered in your mind over the past 45 minutes. You were living in the future, a time period that doesn't exist in your present, and instead of just living in the present and doing your job, you dissociated into a future time that wasn't ever guaranteed in the first place. Throw away your clock, understand that each moment and experience you have moves with the time of life and so you must do the same if you want to fulfill your experiences with elegant happiness.

"Control Is Your Next Step"

Control! Just when you thought you had it all figured out, you are thrown into a pinball machine with no escaping. When life decides to add a cork in your path, you no longer can walk with confidence because you'll never know just how far up ahead the next cork is. Life is full of curve balls, and unpredictable events that force each one of us to be submissive to the power of uncertainty. The only control you can maintain consistently is the literal "next step" your two feet will take. You may not know exactly what manifestations or events will take place within the territory of that "next step", but you certainly can control the physical action of taking it. By doing this you will be proactive in everything you do. If you decide to remain still in the same geographically coordinated location for the rest of your life then you will possess complete control over your entire life simply because your two feet would have never moved. But remaining idle in life is certainly not practical. And so instead, if you make a conscious effort to approach each "next step" with thought then you will control at least where your direct "next step" will take you. And if you always control where your direct "next step" takes you, then you can maintain control over your destiny to some degree.

However, because you don't live alone in this world, sometimes your "next step" is indirectly predetermined by the "next step" of another.   If you decide to push on the gas pedal to advance your car forward, but suddenly the car in front of you pushes on the brake pedal, then you have no choice but to push on the brake pedal as well. In this instance, your original "next step" to move forward was suddenly predetermined by the "next step" of the person in front of you who forced you to slam on the brakes or render your car to an accident. Since you cannot control others and thus their "next step", the best thing to always do is just strictly focus on your "next step" and yourself alone. No one ever forces you to do anything, so only do the things you enjoy and make your "next step" a positive one in a forward progressive direction.

"The Moment Breeds The Experience"

Send yourself off deep into a distant space, a place where no human has gone before. It's dark, it's open, and it's full of enlightenment. This is the power of your mind, for it stretches across a vast sea of infiniteness. Neurons stacked upon neurons compounding into a nest that gives birth to life with broad wings that soar to depths of the unknown consciousness. You must strive each day to find new limits to the creative realm of your imagination. It's a world that only you can create and live in, for it exists in a state composed of a thoughtless matter. Mental atoms crashing into one another, generating a mental image of what is to become your new way of thinking. A way of thinking that can manifest into a thousand other ways of thinking, all within a matter of seconds to then find yourself lost in time and space. And so your time measured in space becomes relative to your recognition of a moment in that time within space, otherwise time does not exist, for it requires the mind's recognition of a designated elapsed amount of seconds to comprehend the number the thoughts one generates within a given moment. And so, you can live more by the moment and less by the time. Tomorrow, when you wake up, take the moment to walk somewhere. As you walk, you realize that within that moment your mind is flowing in a thousand different directions. Even though it is just one moment, you still have single, multiple, and compound thoughts occurring within that one moment. You've reached a certain distance and look back on your traveled path and realize a certain amount of seconds has elapsed, and suddenly you become nauseated for the elapsed time you've lost. But, if the thoughts grounded within that one moment are generated at the same time, then you are living your life by the moment, not by the time. Some moments you have will be special and easily recalled. The uniqueness of these moments parallels the number of neuronal connections established during the occurrence of that moment. Lying in bed ready to fall asleep is rarely a moment you will recall for it bars no impact on your life. But if you could find a way to assign value to each moment, then you could potentially inscribe a mental impact of every moment you have into your mind. In this fashion, every moment you have could be declared unique and special. In life, you want to have a moment and not a moment in time. You want to combine that moment with the right environment. It takes the moment and the environment faceted to your own unique customization to that moment, which will form the experience. The moment is any part of your life that you declare with significance and choose to live within. Thus, the recipe for the perfect moment is the right environment superimposed upon a customizable experience you have in life. Travel the world and shape the things around you into elements that you can incorporate into your life novel. Be for what you are today, and tomorrow will show the experience you desire.

"Love Knows Love"

Did you ever meet someone of the purest mind and heart? I met this woman on a plane. She was in her mid-50s with short red hair, sporting brown leather cowboy boots and a southern accent. This woman spoke with passion for love and all reverence for joy. For two hours straight during our flight home, I listened to her rejoice about what it means to love others, and how truly submitting yourself to love all people of all races and backgrounds can be the most powerful reward in life. I tried diligently to dispel her rationing for peace and happiness and provoked her with ideas of innate qualities of human aggression, pessimism, and struggle. I told her the world we reside in is not exactly balanced, but she incessantly professed that the only balance one needs is that within them self. The true harmony comes when you can give more of yourself than you wish to receive. To go throughout life with the constant expectation of desire and personal wishes is but to only limit your scope of happiness. True happiness comes only to those that tread water and keep their head above the deep sea of temptation. Sin is not foreign to man. But even within a world destined for sin, you can still choose to offer love and it's through the unconditional love for others that you can overcome sin. You cannot remove sin from the world, but you can remove hate through love. If every person woke up tomorrow thinking of ways to love the person next to them on the train, or across the street, or behind the counter, then we could all come together as one species reborn under one new breath. And with this one new breath, we can intake the love of others, systemically interpret it deep within our bodies, and then exhale that converted love into a diffuse form of energy that can be subsequently acquired by someone else. It's the pay it forward cycle, but under the simple deed of love. Cheryl embodied this form of love in every sense of the word. Some may call her crazy, others write her off as an extremist, but to me, Cheryl was simply passionate. I imagine all of us could be reminded of a world that truly can be simple, an agenda of life that truly is pure. The job, the money, the greed and jealousy, the competitive nature of human progression, all fall short of our true vocation to love. The universe was not created unintentionally, and we as humans were not placed here by mistake. We are gifts of a natural biological phenomenon to be shared with one another as gifts around a tree. Share your love and your gifts with the next person and you shall receive the true reward of love. The giver knows not what he gives until he receives that which he does not have.

Δ-Pretend for a moment that you are here. You tilt your head back and give way to the light casted upon your face. You are the breath of energy that forms a breath of happiness and you can share this moment with whomever you choose. Now tilt your head forward and look down at the things beneath you. Encircle yourself in your trust in what you know best and give to those that need your help the most. Choose yourself as a source of reflection for what you would like to know and yield to the power of your mind to guide your inner thoughts to a world unknown. Be for what you know today, and let yourself drift off into a vast, diffuse atmosphere of repose. Find the circle of happiness within the larger circle of nothingness.-Δ